20th Century

Art

Jillian Powell

Wayland

Titles in this series

Art
Cinema
Communications
Farming
Fashion
Medicine
Transport
Warfare

Editors: *Francesca Motisi and Angela Latham*
Designer: *Ross George*

Front cover *Umberto Boccioni's painting* The noise of the street reaches into the house *(1911).*
Back cover *Sculptor Henry Moore at work in his studio.*
Frontispiece *A metal sculpture by Avril Wilson and Lucy Byatt which appeared at the 1988 Brighton Festival. This figure is one of a series of four called the Steel People, and was created as a part of the Travelogue project produced for the Festival by Red Herring Studios.*

First published in 1989 by
Wayland (Publishers) Ltd
61 Western Road, Hove
East Sussex BN3 1JD, England

© Copyright 1989 Wayland (Publishers) Ltd

British Library Cataloguing in Publication Data
Powell, Jillian
Twentieth century art. – (The Twentieth
century).
1. Paintings, 1900–1980 – Critical studies
I. Title II. Series
759.06

ISBN 1–85210–128–8

Typeset by Kalligraphics Ltd, Horley, Surrey,
England
Printed and bound by Sagdos, S.p.A., Milan

Contents

1900–1913 A Changing World

New directions in art	6
Les Fauves	8
Expressionist art in Germany	9

1913–1916 Denial of the Past, Celebration of the Future

Pablo Picasso	14
Futurism celebrates the Modern Age	16
The New York Armory Show	19

1916–1938 Art Between the Wars

Dada	20
Surrealism	23
Salvador Dali	24
Beginnings of Abstraction: Russian Suprematism and Constructivism	26
De Stijl: Neoplasticism	27
Henry Moore and Barbara Hepworth	28

1946–1950 Post-War Art

Abstract Expressionism	32
Rothko's colour field painting	34
Art in Europe	35

1950–1970 Op, Pop and Happenings

Post-Painterly Abstraction	36
Op art	37
Pop art	38
Superrealism	40

1980–1990 Art Today

The Western world	42
The impact of modern art	43
Naïve Painting in Yugoslavia	43
The Mexican muralists	44
Art in Australia	44
African art	45

Glossary	46
Further Reading	47
Index	48

1900-1913

A Changing World

At the turn of the century, Paris, the rich capital city of France, was the centre of the art world. Art reflected a changing world, with young painters and sculptors seeking new subject matter and new sources of inspiration in tribal and folk art.

Above *The hustle and bustle of Paris in 1902: traffic along the Boulevard des Capucines.*

At the turn of the twentieth century, the world was changing fast. In the industrialized countries of the West, many people had moved to the cities to find work in the factories. In their homes, a wide range of new inventions was now having effect. Electric lighting had been introduced (although many homes still relied on gas) and the telephone was in use in major cities. Travel and communications had speeded up, with the motor

car becoming more common on the roads and the first flying machines conquering the skies.

Art, too, was changing. Photography, invented in the first half of the nineteenth century, was forcing painters to look for new directions. If the camera could record places and faces as once only the painter could, what did the painter do now? The cinema, established by 1913, quickly became the most popular form of entertainment, and with grand religious and historical themes no longer seeming relevant to modern life, artists were starting to rethink their subject matter and approach.

From the beginning, twentieth century art was vitally connected to modern life. Research into new fields such as psychology, the science of the mind, by the Austrian psychologist Sigmund Freud, introduced ideas about the subconscious and dream life which encouraged some artists to look inwards for their themes and ideas. Advances such as Einstein's Theory of Relativity were changing people's view of the universe, introducing new ideas and questioning old certainties.

Right A French poster which captures the excitement of the early flying machines.

Below The photographic workshop set up in Reading in 1843 by the pioneer photographer Henry Fox Talbot. By 1900 portrait photography was already well established.

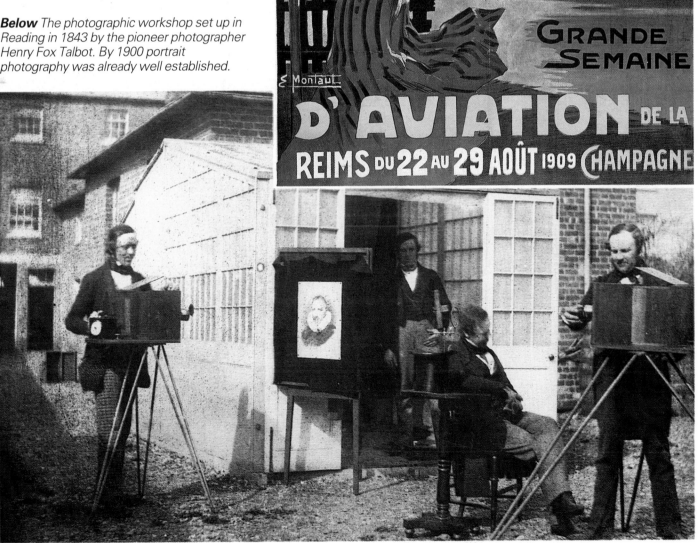

New Directions in Art

Above Landscape with Viaduct: Mont Sainte-Victoire *by Paul Cézanne. Cézanne was born at Aix-en-Provence in the South of France and he painted the nearby Mont Sainte-Victoire many times. He was fascinated by the shape of the mountain, using it to set the interlocking planes of colour into a rhythmic composition.*

In art, too, ideas which had been practised for over 400 years were being challenged. Since the Renaissance, artists had sought to create the appearance of depth in a painting by using the rules of perspective and modelling the figures and objects with light and shadow. The French painter Édouard Manet (1832–83), influenced by Japanese woodblock prints with their flat areas of colour and bold designs, and by the new art of photography, had begun to 'flatten' the picture space. Manet believed that an artist should only paint what he could actually see. He wanted to put what he saw directly onto the canvas, so he painted in broad, lively brushstrokes and fresh colours. He was one of the 'painters of Modern life' that the French poet and critic Baudelaire had been calling for.

Baudelaire said that painters should find their subjects in modern city life and not in ancient history or mythology. Manet wanted to find new techniques to paint these new subjects so he began working directly on to a white-primed canvas rather than in careful layers over a coloured ground as the old masters had done. He was interested in seeing painting as a flat arrangement of shapes and colours, as the Japanese artists had done for centuries. He created patterns from strong colour contrasts and painted without the 'half tones' or greyish colours which Western painters had traditionally used to model form.

Paul Cézanne (1839–1906) went further, inventing a totally new way of organizing a painting. He is sometimes called 'the father of Modern painting'. Like the Impressionist painters, including Monet and Renoir, Cézanne was concerned with painting the truth. The Impressionists painted with small dabs of pure colour to capture light and atmosphere.

Cézanne wanted to go further, seeking beyond what the eye sees to the 'skeleton' of Nature. Realizing that when we look at a landscape our eye moves and does not stay at one fixed point, Cézanne tried to imitate the moving viewpoint. He reduced the shapes of trees, mountains and houses to simple geometrical forms – cylinders, spheres and cones – then rearranged them into composition built with short, square blocks of colour.

Left Manet's Piper (1866) was rejected by the Paris Salon because it appeared so flat, almost like a cut-out or a playing card. Manet creates a bold outline, using strong colours against a flat background.

Below Sailing boats at Aria, *by the Japanese print master Hiroshige (1797–1858) shows the bold design and colours that influenced Western artists including Manet. Hiroshige concentrates on the patterns made by the sails in the wind, using flat areas of intense colour.*

In 1904, a large exhibition of Cézanne's works was shown in Paris, which, due to the work of the Impressionists and the Post-Impressionists had become the centre of the art world. Young painters like Pablo Picasso and Henri Matisse living there in the early years of the century, became active in establishing new movements which set the course of twentieth century art. The movements shared a common interest in seeking new sources of inspiration, especially in ethnic and folk art.

Right *Henri Matisse in his studio in Paris, 1909. Matisse is now considered the 'old master' of modern art, but critics of the day attacked his style as 'the barbaric and naïve sport of a child who plays with the box of colours he just got as a Christmas present.'*

Expressionist Art in Germany

In Germany, a group calling itself *Die Brücke*, or The Bridge, looked to late medieval German woodcuts and primitive woodcarvings for inspiration. They revived the use of woodcut in strong, crudely carved images which expressed their own frustration and desire for change.

The Bridge was founded in Dresden in 1905 by a group of four young architects, including Ernst Kirchner (1880–1938).

They were the first artists to choose their own name (seeing themselves as a bridge between the old and the new) and published their ideas in a manifesto. Their work was Expressionist, using strong colours, violent brushwork and distorted, harsh forms to convey their inner feelings and emotions. Any work which uses distorted forms and colours to express the artist's emotions may be termed Expressionist.

Above *A woodcut from* Die Brücke *manifesto by Kirchner.*

Van Gogh's paintings are Expressionist, as are those of the Norwegian painter Edvard Munch (1863–1944). The Expressionist works of The Bridge convey a sense of unease and frustration. These artists were concerned with the role art could play in changing society, and they wanted to achieve freedom on every level, personal, political and artistic.

Another group fighting for the freedom to experiment was *Der Blaue Reiter*, or The Blue Rider, founded in Munich in 1911 by the Russian painter Wassily Kandinsky (1866–1944) and the German Franz Marc (1880–1916). They wanted to be free of the conventions which had shaped European art for centuries, and they believed that to be creative, an artist must destroy established values and start anew. Kandinsky's friend, the composer Schönberg, was pursuing the same ideas in music. The Blue Rider looked for inspiration to folk and naïve painting,

African and Oceanic art, and art produced by children and the mentally ill also provided inspiration. Like The Bridge, they were Expressionist artists, wanting their paintings to express their inner feelings. Rapid communications opening up in the twentieth century meant that there was a constant exchange of ideas between the different groups, and *Der Blaue Reiter* was aware of, and responded to, the ideas of two major movements which emerged in the first decade of the new century – Cubism and Futurism.

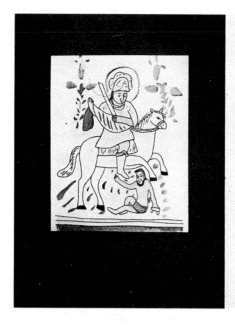 

DER BLAUE REITER

HERAUSGEBER: KANDINSKY
FRANZ MARC

MÜNCHEN, R. PIPER & CO. VERLAG, 1912

Right *The 1912 manifesto of* Der Blaue Reiter *showing the horseman who became the group's emblem. The group took its name from the title of a painting by Kandinsky. They sought to express the spiritual side of people, which they felt had been neglected by the impressionists.*

Below *In* Horse in a Landscape, *Franz Marc uses areas of rich colour and shapes, like the arc of the horse's neck, to create movement.*

Denial of the Past, Celebration of the Future

Picasso's revolutionary painting *Les Demoiselles d'Avignon* broke centuries-old traditions and introduced Cubism. In Italy, a group calling themselves the Futurists celebrated the Modern Age. But in America, Modern art was ridiculed at the New York Armory Show of 1913.

For 400 years, since the Italian Renaissance, artists had tried to mirror the real world. But by the nineteenth century, there was already a growing belief in the artists' freedom to express their own thoughts and ideas. The Symbolist painters had begun to explore their own dreams, fantasies and imagination. Romantic painters communi-cated their feelings through colour, design and brushwork. At the turn of the century, when African masks were first displayed in Europe, the powerful forms of ethnic and folk art inspired new ways of looking at things. This change in approach was dramatically illustrated by one painting – Picasso's *Les Demoiselles d'Avignon*.

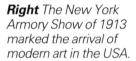
Right *The New York Armory Show of 1913 marked the arrival of modern art in the USA.*

By 1906, when he began painting Les Demoiselles d'Avignon, *the twenty-five year-old Pablo Picasso was a successful painter in Paris. He made over thirty sketches and chose a canvas over two metres square for this major work, which in 1907 shocked even his most devoted admirers.*

In subject, Picasso's five nude figures recalled earlier paintings of bathers, but the artist had broken the human body up into angular planes and wedges. One critic said the painting resembled a field of broken glass. Ears have been discarded, eyes placed at different levels, and noses pulled into profile. The figure at the lower right-hand corner is so distorted that her face and back are both visible. Two of the figures wear barbaric masks marked with slashes which were inspired by Picasso's study of tribal masks and ancient sculpture from his native Spain. Picasso's treatment of space, too, was revolutionary, with the figures flattened against the surface and little sense of depth.

Above left *An African Bakongo tribal mask showing the simple, hollowed shapes and 'reeding' (incised lines) which influenced Picasso's Demoiselles d'Avignon.*

Above *Pablo Picasso: Les Demoiselles d'Avignon (1907).*

Left *Georges Braque: Maisons à L'Estaque.*

Among those who were shocked by this painting was the French painter Georges Braque (1882–1963). The following summer, however, he went to L'Estaque, a picturesque fishing village on the outskirts of Marseilles, and painted a series of works which show Picasso's influence.

In Braque's *Maisons à L'Estaque*, objects are reduced to simple blocks of colour. Houses have been stripped of doors and windows, tree trunks reduced to simple cylinders and foliage to flat areas of green.

When the painting was exhibited with five others at Kahnweiler's gallery in Paris, the critic Vauxcelles wrote scornfully that Braque had 'reduced everything – skies, figures and houses – to cubes.' As Picasso and Braque explored their new style further, the name Cubist caught on.

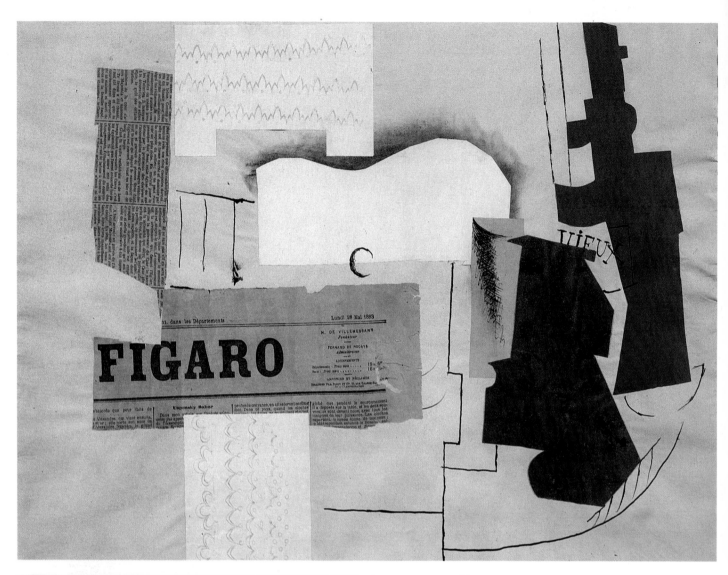

Above *In* Guitar, Newspaper, Wine Glass and Bottle *(1913) Picasso reinterprets a still life subject using a mixture of collage cut-outs and painting or drawing. In this way, a traditional subject is treated in an original manner.*

Left *Picasso photographed in his Paris studio by Lee Miller, in 1909.*

Pablo Picasso

Picasso, born in Spain in 1881, was one of the greatest artists and personalities of the century. In his long career (he died in 1973) he embraced every theme from still life painting to the horrors of war. His huge mural painting, Guernica, *was painted in 1937 in response to the ruthless destruction of the Spanish Civil War. Picasso also experimented with etching and lithography which have both become popular forms of print-making in the twentieth century.*

At first the Cubists concentrated on still-life subjects – bottles, guitars, wineglasses – painting them in drab greys, browns and ochres, with all interest focused on the way many different views of an object could be represented in one image. From about 1911 Cubism entered a new phase, called Collage or Synthetic Cubism. (From these Cubist beginnings, Collage became a popular form of twentieth century art.) Picasso and Braque pasted a variety of materials on to the surface of their canvases – stencils of letters, words and numbers, fabrics and sand. In places they faked textures like wood grain. In doing so, they were questioning, 'What is art? What is reality?'

Cubist works were shown in cities like London, New York and Amsterdam, and Cubist ideas were quickly taken up by other artists including Juan Gris, Fernand Léger and Robert Delaunay.

In sculpture, Picasso introduced new materials and techniques, often using bits of junk like the parts of a push-bike which he used to suggest a bull's head. Other sculptors, like Jacob Epstein (1880–1959) and Constantin Brancusi (1876–1957), shared Picasso's enthusiasm for African tribal art, and worked towards simplified forms using traditional methods of direct carving from stone or casting in bronze.

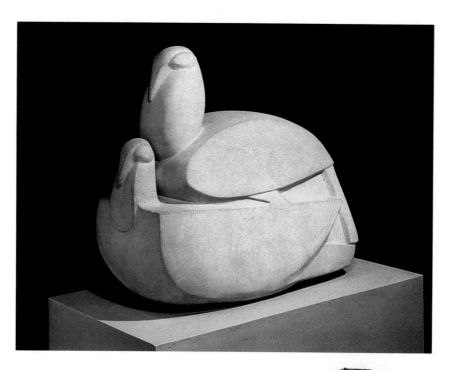

Above Sir Jacob Epstein's Doves *show the influence of the ancient and primitive carvings the sculptor studied at the Louvre Museum in Paris.*

Right Brancusi's Endless Column *(1918) suggests a living, growing form and reminds us of tribal totem poles.*

Below Picasso's Guernica, *reproduced on a Spanish postage stamp.*

correos
ESPAÑA 200 PTA
GUERNICA. PABLO RUIZ PICASSO   F.N.M.T. 1981

Futurism Celebrates the Modern Age

During this period, the paintings of Picasso, the music of Igor Stravinsky and the advance of modern technology all seemed to be leading to a new, exciting era. A group of artists working in Italy set out to capture the energy and excitement of modern life in works which celebrated machinery, movement, power and speed. The Futurists, led by the poet Filippo Marinetti and including the painters Umberto Boccioni, Gino Severini and Giacomo Balla, set down their ideas in two manifestos, published in 1910, and staged their first exhibition in Paris in 1912. At the time Filippo Marinetti said, 'A racing car, its frame adorned with great pipes like snakes with explosive breath, is more beautiful than the Victory of Samothrace,' (a famous Classical Greek sculpture).

Faster travel and communications meant that Futurist ideas spread quickly across Europe. In Britain, the Vorticists, a group centred around Wyndham Lewis (1884–1957) pursued similar aims, trying to extract the essence of the 'vortex' or whirling force of twentieth century life. Their first, and last, exhibition was in 1915.

In Italy, the Futurist movement had political as well as artistic aims, and demanded changes not just in the visual arts, but in the whole of Italian culture and life. They believed in progress at all costs, and thought that even violence and conflict were desirable where they achieved change. 'Beauty', they said, 'exists only in struggle.'

Below In Abstract Speed, the Car has Passed *(1913) Balla creates an impression of movement and excitement through interlocking planes of bright colour.*

Above A poster advertising the Fiat factory at Turin which captures the sense of wonder at the power and strength of the new motor cars and flying machines. Marinetti lived nearby at Milan, the industrial capital of Italy.

Right The poet Filippo Marinetti photographed in his motor car, c.1908.

Some Futurist painters, however, were more concerned with the visual challenge of representing energy and movement. The photographer Eadward Muybridge had already developed the technique of taking a sequence of still photographs in quick succession. Futurists like Balla and Boccioni used a variety of different devices to capture movement, showing several stages of motion in one figure, and breaking colour into small patches.

The New York Armory Show

By 1910, improving communications meant that the new ideas of the modern movements had spread across Europe. But it was at the 1913 Armory Show in New York that the new European art, including Cubist and Fauvist works, was first seen in America. The public and critics were outraged by what they saw, and at the centre of the scandal was Marcel Duchamp's Nude Descending a Staircase No. 2. Duchamp's work contains elements of both Cubism and Futurism, showing a female figure moving downstairs in a series of interlocking planes, wedges and dotted lines. The public were shocked that a traditional subject, the female nude, could be treated this way, and the painting was ridiculed as an example of 'the craziness of modern art.'

Right Nude Descending a Staircase No. 2 (1912) by Marcel Duchamp.

Left Workshop (1914–15) by Percy Wyndham Lewis. Busy lines and spiralling shapes make us feel as if we are falling into a 'vortex'.

SEEING NEW YORK WITH A CUBIST

FUTURIST ART INCLUDED IN STATE VICE INQUIRY

Investigator Finds Nude Pictures at Institute Attracting Gaze of Young Girls

CUBIST ART IS HERE AS CLEAR AS MUD

If You Don't Know What It Is Just Read This and Never Worry Again.

CUBIST ART BAFFLES CROWD

Diagram No Aid to Seeing 'Nude' Descend Staircase.

Left and above Newspaper cuttings of the time reflect the public reaction to the Armory Show.

1916-1938

Art Between the Wars

The First World War (1914–18) resulted in widespread destruction and loss of life, shattering many people's faith in the Modern Age. Two groups emerged in response to the horrors of war. Dada set out to mock and destroy the values of the established order which had failed. The Surrealists searched their own dreams and subconscious. Artists continued to turn away from nature, and some abandoned recognizable subjects to explore the pure qualities of abstract art – colour, line and shape.

Dada

The optimism expressed by the Futurists was shattered by the horrors of the First World War. Thousands of young men lost their lives in the mud and the chaos of trench warfare, and people faced the destructive potential of new weaponry. Many people felt the world had gone mad, and especially among the young there was a distrust of the past and of the values of a society which had come close to destroying itself.

Below Soldiers on the Western Front during the First World War, which claimed so many lives.

Above (left) The poet Tristan Tzara (1896–1963) and (right) the painter Francis Picabia (1879–1953).

Right A lithograph broadsheet advertising a Dada evening at the Hague.

At a café in Zurich, a group of young artists including the painter Jean (Hans) Arp (1887–1966) and the poet Tristan Tzara, founded Dada – a movement which set out to attack the established values of art and society. At about the same time, a second group was forming in New York, including Marcel Duchamp, Francis Picabia and the painter and photographer Man Ray.

Dada – a nonsense name meaning hobby-horse in French – was an attitude affecting all the arts, and life itself, rather than a style. Marcel Duchamp (1887–1968) summed up the Dadaists' rebellious attitude to the past when he painted a moustache and beard on to a print of the *Mona Lisa*, Leonardo da Vinci's famous Renaissance masterpiece.

Duchamp challenged accepted views on art by exhibiting 'ready-mades', objects like a bottle-rack which he simply signed with his own or a false name. He made fun of people who merely admired a work of art for its famous signature.

The Dadaist Jean (Hans) Arp made 'chance' collages, throwing pieces of paper onto a support and pasting them where they landed. Kurt Schwitters (1887–1948) used junk like old bus tickets, cartons and torn newspapers to make collages and construct sculptures. Dada set out to shock – at the first Dada exhibition, viewers were even offered axes so they could chop up any of the works they didn't like!

Right Picture with Spatial Growths – Picture with Two Small Dogs *(1929–30). A mixed media collage in which Schwitters uses old envelopes, calendar pages, tickets and newspapers.*

Surrealism

One of the organizers of the first Dada exhibition, Max Ernst (1891–1976), later moved to Paris where he, Hans Arp and Francis Picabia (1879–1953) became involved with founding a new movement – Surrealism. Ernst had become interested in the art produced by the mentally insane when he was at university in Bonn. In the first decades of the twentieth century, the theories of the Austrian psychologist Sigmund Freud were becoming widely known, encouraging a growing interest in the way our subconscious mind, dreams and fantasies control our behaviour.

In Paris, the Surrealists experimented with new techniques of discovering images hidden in the subconscious. Methods such as automatic drawing (like doodling) were used to suggest ideas for paintings, and new sources of imagery were explored: the strange, biomorphic shapes of micro-organisms revealed by science, the grotesque forms of modern machinery, the power of primitive art and art produced by the mentally insane. Like Dada, the Surrealist movement was far-reaching, affecting art, literature, ballet, design and films in the inter-war years in Europe.

Surrealism means 'above' or 'beyond' realism, and allowed the painter to explore the odd and the irrational. The Belgian Surrealist René Magritte (1898–1967) often used size or scale to surprise the viewer, painting an apple filling a room, for example, or odd combinations like a man wearing a bowler hat with a white bird obscuring his face. Joan Miró (1893–1985) had studied the paintings of children and primitive peoples, and he experimented with simple primary colours and delicate lines, incorporating floating words and phrases to conjure up his own whimsical fantasies.

Above The spirit of Dada: a woman with a mask of flowers photographed in London's Trafalgar Square to publicize the 1936 International Surrealist exhibition.

Above A fantasy photograph captures Dali!

Left Exterior of the Dali Museum-Theatre at Figueras, in Spain.

Salvador Dali

One of the most flamboyant Surrealist painters was the Spanish eccentric, Salvador Dali (1904–1989). He worked in many media – painting, writing, film and jewellery. He was expelled from Madrid art school in 1926 for 'extravagant behaviour' and throughout his life he was a showman. (He turned up at the London Surrealist exhibition in 1936 wearing a diver's suit!) In his strange, nightmarish visions, nothing appears solid: one thing melts into another. Dali painted his own visions, fantasies and hallucinations, using a masterful technique to achieve a glassy, polished surface which adds to the eeriness of his paintings.

Left The Dadaist group, painted by Max Ernst (1922). The artists' names appear to the left and right of the painting.

Below Painting 1927 by Miró. With a flick of the brush or a dash of colour, Miró creates liveliness and humour. The intense blue background gives a feeling of space.

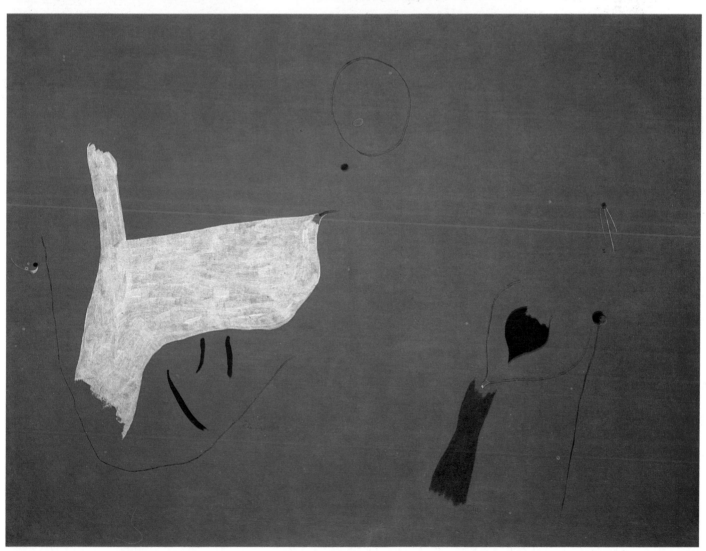

Beginnings of Abstraction: Russian Suprematism and Constructivism

Right *Tatlin at work on the model for his 'Tower,' the design for a giant building.*

Below *Shapes, lines and primary colours –* Suprematist Painting *(1915) by Malevich.*

Miró's work was moving away from figures and objects towards pure shapes, lines and colours. As artists turned away from nature, some were abandoning recognizable subjects to see if painting could work more directly on our senses, as music does.

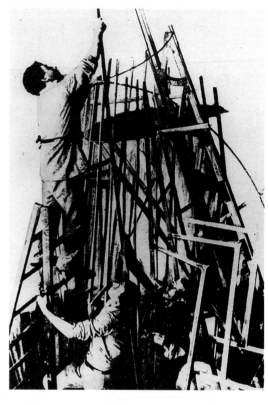

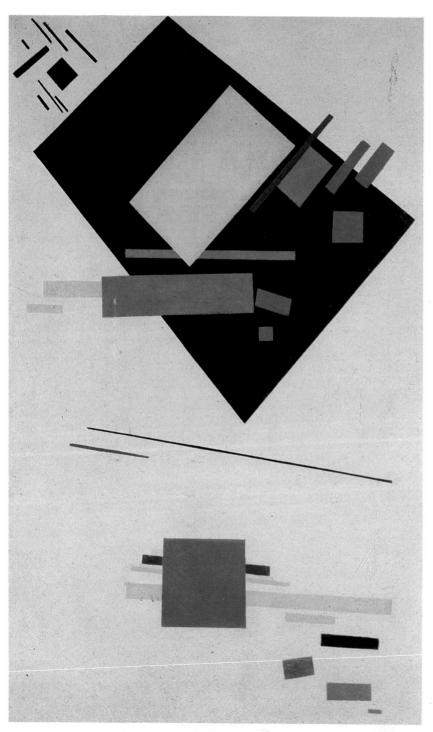

The first 'abstract' paintings were produced by the Russian artist Wassily Kandinsky around 1911. Kandinsky had been a member of the Blue Rider group in Germany, and had come into contact with the Cubists and the Futurists before he returned to Russia. There he found that a group of artists, including Kasimir Malevich, Vladimir Tatlin and Naum Gabo, were already producing abstract works. The Russian Suprematists, as they were called, wanted painting to express 'pure artistic feeling' through geometric shapes and colours. In 1913, Tatlin went to Paris. The Cubist Collage works he saw there inspired him to construct models in relief, later experimenting with constructions in glass, metal and wood. These became the basis of the movement, Constructivism, in which Tatlin worked with Gabo and Antoine Pevsner.

The Russian Constructivists were opposed to illusion in art and wanted to use 'real materials' and 'real space'. Some sought to create socially 'useful' art with posters, propaganda literature and industrial design.

De Stijl: Neoplasticism

The work of the Russian Suprematists influenced the Dutch painter and theorist Theo van Doesburg (1883–1931) who with Piet Mondrian (1872–1944) founded the *De Stijl* movement in Holland in 1917. In the *De Stijl* magazine published that year, van Doesburg and Mondrian set down their ideas for a new abstract style which they called Neoplasticism. They wanted to be 'truly Modern artists' and to encourage a new awareness of beauty.

Van Doesburg and Mondrian believed that the precision of the new machine technology was better than individual craftsmanship, and that humankind was entering a new age in which order was all-important. Modern artists, they said, should express this order through the 'new' plasticism, which meant rejecting art as representation and restricting their means of expression. Artists should limit themselves to straight lines and right angles, and to the primary colours or the 'non-colours', white, black and grey.

The *De Stijl* magazine was the most influential of all the new journals which were set up after the First World War. Neoplasticist ideas spread outside the Netherlands, influencing fine art, architecture and interior design in many European countries and in America where Mondrian settled in 1940. The style inspired the design of everything from posters and packaging to curtains and linoleum flooring.

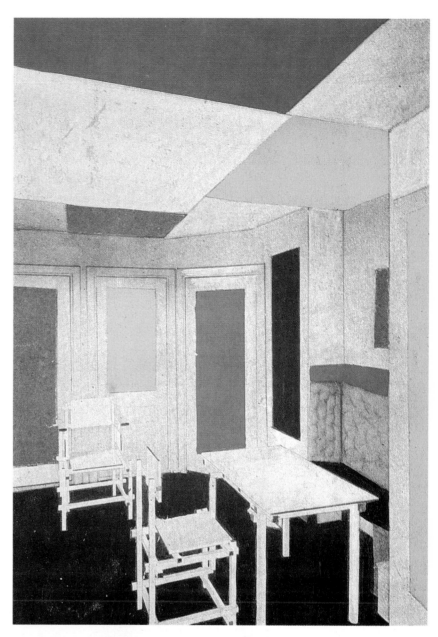

Above *Theo van Doesburg's design for an interior.*

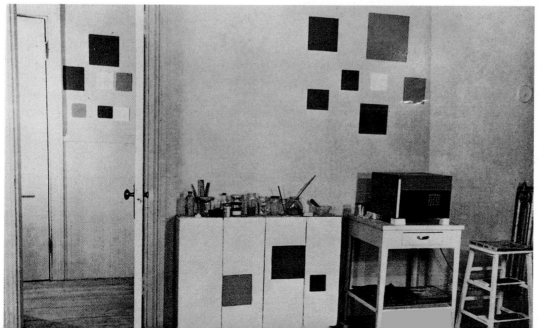

Left *Mondrian's last studio in New York, showing how geometric shapes were used to define space.*

Above Reclining Figure (1951) by Henry Moore. In Moore's sculptures the spaces are as important as the mass or volume of the stone or bronze.

Henry Moore and Barbara Hepworth

Just as painters were looking to new sources for inspiration, sculptors were finding new directions. The British sculptor Henry Moore, born in Yorkshire in 1898 (died 1985), studied the art of ancient cultures, especially those of Pre-Columbian Mexico and West Africa, as well as the great European Masters like Michelangelo. He was particularly interested in sculptures that reflected a role in nature, such as Aztec images of the rain god who was believed to water the crops. Like the Surrealists, Moore believed that the artist's hand could be guided by the subconscious, and he collected rocks, bones, pebbles and driftwood, basing sculptures on the forms these 'accidents' of nature suggested to him.

As official war artist during the Second World War (1939–45) Moore made numerous drawings of figures huddled in bomb shelters, and these later inspired some of his massive sculptures in wood, bronze and stone. These works transform the human body into monumental forms suggestive of waterworn rocks and caves. He returned again and again to themes of reclining figures or mother and child, seeking forms which have a vitality of their own, rather than conventional beauty. Holes and spaces are as important in Moore's work as solid forms, and this is true of the work of another Yorkshire-born sculptor, Barbara Hepworth (1903–75).

Barbara Hepworth found her inspiration in the rocks, foliage and shell creatures of the English Channel coastline and the Cornish countryside. Many of her sculptures, like Moore's, were created for open-air settings, and suggest natural pebble or rock forms, with their curvilinear oval and spiral shapes and holes. Like Moore, Hepworth used traditional methods of casting in bronze, or direct carving from wood and stone, sometimes using strings, which she said represented 'the tension I feel between myself and the sea, the wind and the hills.'

Below Stringed Figure (Curlew) Version II *(1956)* by Barbara Hepworth.

Post-War Art

The Second World War (1939–45) saw the rise of power of the USA and New York became the centre of the art world. Jackson Pollock invented 'Action Painting' and the canvas became 'an arena in which to act.' In Europe artists explored, in either the abstract or the figurative tradition, their visions and experiences of a war-torn world.

Right *Nazi War poster: the force from which artists and others were fleeing.*

Below *European emigrants arriving in New York, seeing the famous skyline for the first time.*

The Second World War marked a watershed, heralding the age of the atomic bomb and rapid advances in science, technology and communications. The experience of war, with the horrors of the Blitzkrieg and the Nazi concentration camps, was reflected in the works of artists who no longer considered beauty essential to art.

DER SIEG WIRD UNSER SEIN!

Painters continued to reject nature, using crowded, abstract forms, unexpected viewpoints and harsh colours to express their sense of a violent and restless age.

Two World Wars saw the rapid rise to power of the USA, a country that is rich in natural resources and labour force. During the 1930s, many artists and teachers had left Europe for the USA, and as they settled, New York became a new artistic centre.

Among those who settled in the USA were the Surrealists Max Ernst, Yves Tanguy and André Breton. Under their influence, young American painters began to combine a Surrealist approach to space and form with an expressive, even aggressive use of paint. There was an openness, too, to different influences, Eastern art and culture as well as Western, American Indian and Pre-Columbian.

Above *Artists in exile: photograph taken at an exhibition at a New York gallery in 1942. The artists include Max Ernst (fourth from left, first row) and Piet Mondrian (second from left, second row).*

Abstract Expressionism

Jackson Pollock (1912–56) was the first American painter to begin an international art movement – Abstract Expressionism. Pollock had studied the work of Cézanne, Picasso and Kandinsky, and had experimented with the Cubist style. But he was also drawn to the bold and powerful forms of primitive art, like the sand paintings of the American Navajo tribe, which were created on the ground in a kind of ritual ceremony. Like the Surrealists, Pollock was interested in primitive art because of its direct contact with the subconscious, and he was influenced, too, by the vast mural paintings of Mexican Revolutionary painters like Diego Rivera, with their expressive, often violent use of paint.

By 1947, Pollock had developed the 'drip and splash' style of Action Painting which made him the leader of the new Abstract Expressionist movement. Instead of using a traditional easel, he laid his canvases on the floor, pouring and dripping paint from a can as he moved over and around the surface. Paint was trailed, dribbled and splashed to express the artist's every gesture and movement, then worked with trowels, sticks and knives, sometimes with sand, broken glass or other matter added to create rich surface textures. The design had no relationship to the shape or size of the canvas, and Pollock would paint continuous compositions, later cutting off the canvas where he chose. Pollock's works were painted on an enormous scale, intended to surround and involve the spectator.

Although Abstract Expressionism drew elements from the major European movements – Expressionism, Cubism, Surrealism – the American painters worked on a huge scale and devised revolutionary methods of paint application. Among these painters, besides Pollock, were William de Kooning, Franz Kline and Mark Rothko.

Opposite *Jackson Pollock at work in his studio. He once said 'My painting is direct. . .I want to express my feelings rather than illustrate them'.*

Below *The sacred ceremony of sand painting practised by the American Indian Navajo tribe.*

Rothko's Colour Field Painting

Below *Mark Rothko's Light Red Over Black (1957). Rothko admired the works of the great landscape painter J.M.W. Turner, whose misty distances are echoed in Rothko's floating, dissolving colours.*

Rothko was born in Russia in 1903 but had settled in the USA when he was only ten years old. In the 1940s and 1950s, he and a number of other leading artists began experimenting with the use of flat areas of colour designed to bring the viewer into an almost trance-like state of contemplation. Rothko used powerful, resonant colours and large, simple shapes which seemed to float in coloured space. Many people saw these strong visual statements as carrying some

kind of religious or spiritual meaning, conveying a sense of despair in a world which, since the splitting of the atom, was under threat of total destruction.

Artists like Mark Rothko and Jackson Pollock represented a new kind of artist. Pollock had won fame quickly, was an alcoholic, and a legend by the time of his death in a car crash at the age of forty-four. Rothko suffered deep depressions, and committed suicide at the age of sixty-seven.

Above *Mark Rothko.*

Below *In the Liverpool Tate Gallery, Rothko's paintings hang as the artist directed. In this picture you can see the scale of his work.*

Art in Europe

The New York School of painters had a far-reaching influence, promoting the idea of painting as a process of self-discovery by the artist. After the Second World War had ended, some European refugees had returned to Europe to settle. A number of artists were working with interests similar to the Abstract Expressionists. The German-born painter Wols (Wolfgang Schulze) (1913–51) had begun painting spontaneously, with densely-worked paint textures, during the war. He once described his work as 'drawing flowing from the fingers'. In France, the painter George Mathieu (1921–) was painting in spontaneous splashes, with paint smeared from the tube and worked freely with the fingers in an all-over manner and on a scale similar to Pollock's. He wanted to create through his vast abstract works a new 'epic' painting.

Other artists responded to the anxieties and uncertainties of the Post-War era by working within the figurative rather than the abstract tradition. The Italian sculptor Alberto Giacometti (1901–66) had worked in the Cubist, Constructivist and Surrealist styles but in the years following the Second World War, he developed his most distinctive style. His frail, elongated figures look isolated even in a crowd, and their skeletal forms seem to express the loneliness and despair of the Modern Age.

In the work of the British painter Francis Bacon (1909–) the violence and suffering of life in the twentieth century are expressed in brutal, distorted forms. Bacon takes a traditional image like Velasquez' calm and dignified portrait of Pope Innocent X, and transforms it into a series of screaming popes, more suggestive of madness than control. Along with Giacometti, Bacon reasserted the figurative tradition, but his interpretation has little to do with traditional Renaissance ideals of calm, order and balance.

Below Study for a Pope (1955, 152.5 × 117cm) by Francis Bacon.

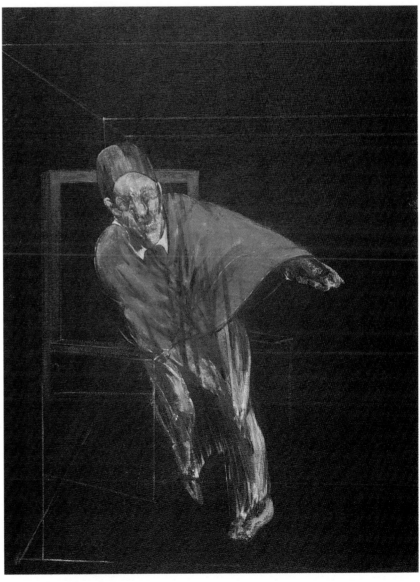

Op, Pop and Happenings

By the mid 1950s, the economic and social climate of the Western world was changing rapidly. The Post-War boom – a period of economic growth and reconstruction – began to make itself felt in the rich capital cities of Europe and the USA. Art and the media reflected a new emphasis on the material comforts of a consumer society.

Right A student working on a sculpture in the Royal College of Art (1966).

Below In Drought (1962) Noland concentrates on the precise geometry of concentric circles, using acrylic paints on canvas.

Post-Painterly Abstraction

In New York and London, a new generation of artists began to react against the Expressionist art of the New York School, including the Americans Frank Stella (1936–) and Kenneth Noland (1924–). They did so by

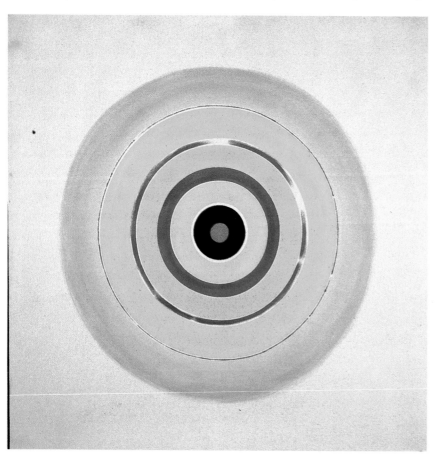

rejecting the expressive brushwork and spontaneous approach of the Abstract Expressionists in favour of carefully planned, mathematically controlled images based on graded squares and circles. This new style of Post-Painterly Abstraction cultivated an almost machine-made look, with flat areas of bright colour precisely painted in enamel or metallic paints.

Left British painter Bridget Riley working in her studio.

Below The Tinguely Fountain, *Basel, Switzerland, showing the 'kinetic' use of water power.*

Op Art

Some European painters like Bridget Riley (1931–) and Victor Vasarely (1908–) explored the Post-Painterly trend by using geometric patterns or wavy lines and dazzling fluorescent colours to give the illusion of the image forming and re-forming before our eyes. Some artists went on to experiment with real movement, using moving parts which might be set in motion either by air currents or machinery or by a spectator. Clockwork, springs, water power and motors were all used to create moving or 'Kinetic' art, which like Op art, reflected the trend towards art becoming a form of public entertainment, linked with modern décor, fashion and films.

Pop Art

Artists were rethinking the role of art in a technological age, and there was a growing feeling that art was only valid if it could be mass-produced, or communicated through modern mass communications. One image, a collage produced by the British artist Richard Hamilton (1922–) entitled '*Just what is it that makes today's homes so different, so appealing?*' seemed to capture the spirit of the moment.

In Hamilton's collage, the cinema, tape recorder, television advertisement, even the tin of ham, are the 'stuff' of twentieth century life, reflecting Western wealth and materialism. Hamilton is both celebrating modern life and making fun of it through his odd assembly of people and objects.

Pop art like this caught on quickly in London and the USA, seeking its inspiration in the popular culture of films, cartoons, posters, packaging, pop music and science fiction. Artists like David Hockney (1937–) in Britain and Andy Warhol (1930–87) in America, acquired pop-star status, and with individuals and corporations rich from business and ready to spend money on modern art, art itself became an industry.

Pop art was intended to appeal to ordinary men and women and to the young in particular. Like comic strip cartoons and the Teddy-boy culture, it may be seen as part of a wider revolt against 'the establishment'.

Right *Richard Hamilton's* Just What Is It That Makes Today's Homes So Different, So Appealing? *(1956). Hamilton uses a collage technique, combining mass produced images cut out from magazines to make an original work.*

For Andy Warhol, it was throw-away objects such as the soup can or the Pepsi bottle which expressed the modern age. He used methods like silk-screen printing which allowed him to repeat an image, such as that of a famous personality like Marilyn Monroe, with only slight variations in the printing. Roy Lichtenstein (1923–) took individual frames from comic strip cartoons, blowing them up and colouring them using a stencil method which echoed the cheap printing methods of the originals.

While painters worked in flat, sharp colours using modern tools like the airbrush, sculptors used materials like plaster, plastics and fibreglass. They assembled 'boxes' or 'environments', using found objects in a life-size setting. The Scottish-born sculptor Eduardo Paolozzi (1924–) used casts of pieces of machinery and fragments of mechanical junk to construct heavy, mechanistic sculptures which might then be brightly painted.

All these experimental works reflected the new freedom which affected art, fashion, manners and morals in the 1960s. The younger generation wanted to break barriers in every field, and in art this resulted in an urge to free painting from the frame and the wall. Artists like Yves Klein, Joseph Beuys, and Allan Kaprow performed Happenings, presenting art as a theatrical

experience or event, which might take place anywhere – in a department store, a gymnasium or a car park. Junk, live models and sounds might all be used to convey the artist's message. Happenings became popular in Europe, the USA and Japan, and gave rise to today's Performance Art.

Superrealism

In the late 1960s and early 1970s, a new international movement, Superrealism, emerged. In Europe and the USA, artists developed techniques of painting reality in precise, even strangely heightened, detail. Some, like the American Chuck Close (1940–) used the technique for portraiture, painting vast portrait heads, two metres or more in height, from blown-up photographs, using acrylic paints applied with an airbrush. The British-born painter Malcolm Morley (1931–) who had settled in New York in 1964, applied the same exacting realism to landscape and city scenes. In the 1960s he began working from the bright, clear images on postcards and travel brochures. His paintings of this period are surrounded by white borders to help make them look two dimensional.

Superrealist sculptors like John de Andrea (1941–) and Duane Hanson (1925–) created uncannily life-like figures using painted fibreglass or plastics, real hair and clothes. With their garish clothes and bland expressions, Hanson's figures can be disturbing. They seem to express the loneliness of today's city life and suggest the emptiness of a life devoted to material possessions.

Opposite *Duane Hanson Traveller with Sunburn (1986), oil-painted bronze and mixed media.*

Below *Malcolm Morley The S. S. Amsterdam in front of Rotterdam (1966). Morley was fascinated by boats and the sea from his childhood.*

Art Today

Ours is the age of the computer, of satellite communications, space travel and the atomic bomb. Technology continues to change our lifestyles, and art continues to reflect this change.

Below The hummingbird figure has become the most well known of all Nazca lines for its beautiful design.

The Western World

In recent years, there has been a dramatic increase in the variety of media available to the artist – from synthetic-based paints, fibreglass and plastics, to lasers, video and holograms. Throughout the twentieth century artists have been asking the question 'What is art?' Today they explore that question freely, experimenting with modern materials and new techniques such as airbrush painting, silk-screen printing and welding sculpture. Increasingly they ignore or blur distinctions between painting and sculpture, and between art and life. Canvases are stretched into three-dimensional shapes, life-size fibreglass figures are placed in real settings, and 'installation pieces' include real objects such as a television set or a ringing telephone.

The Happenings of the 1960s have survived as Performance art. Some Performance artists have branched into 'Body art', using their own bodies as subject matter, and recording their actions in photographs or on film. Photography itself has become an important art form in the twentieth century (sometimes with a written commentary added), as have printmaking techniques like silk-screen and lithography. Photography has also been used to record the work of Earth or Land artists who use the land itself for large scale projects which make us look afresh at the shapes and ideas suggested by our environment. The work of Land artists like Robert Smithson, Carl Andre and Walter de Maria reflects the continuing preoccupation of this century with the powerful forms of primitive art, in particular, pre-historic sites like the mysterious ancient tracks in the Nazca valley, Peru.

The Impact of Modern Art

Throughout the century, Europe and the USA have continued to dominate the art world. But modern travel and communications have meant that the impact of the major modern movements has been felt in Africa and Central America, and in countries like Australia and Japan. In some cases, the spread of Western ideas has tended to suppress indigenous traditions; in others, native traditions have been combined with the new ideas. Folk art, too, has flourished, yet another aspect of twentieth century art which is spontaneous, imaginative and unhindered by convention.

Above and left *The Land artist Christo (1935–) uses 'Packaging art', wrapping walls or buildings in plastic or canvas to make us see familiar structures afresh.*

^{footer}

Above *Diego Rivera working in his studio.*

Below *Sidney Nolan's* Ned Kelly on a Dromedary *shows the artist's powerful naïve style, with his subject set against a stark desert landscape.*

The Mexican Muralists

One school of painters that attracted the attention of American and European painters in the Post-War period was the Mexican Muralists. After the Mexican Revolution of 1910, the Socialist government commissioned artists like Diego Rivera, David Siqueiros and José Orozco to paint vast murals celebrating the ideals of the Revolution in public places such as state or commercial buildings. Mural painting on a large scale was rooted in Pre-Columbian art, but the Mexican painters used their bold, dramatic style to express social and political themes of the day.

Diego Rivera (1886–1957) had lived in Paris from 1911–21 and had been associated with the Cubist painters. On his return to Mexico in 1921, he combined his knowledge of Modern European art with a study of Mexican folk art, developing a bold, direct style to deal with themes like the power of the work-force and the destruction of special privilege and poverty under the Revolutionary regime.

One of the painters who was politically active, David Siqueiros (1896–1974), had been in Paris with Rivera in 1819. On his return to Mexico, he combined his knowledge of Mexican folklore with a Surrealist approach, and incorporated modern techniques like drip painting, photo-montage and airbrushing. The distorted, Expressionist forms and multiple viewpoints of his vast murals convey a powerful drama which was designed to teach Revolutionary ideals to a population that was largely illiterate.

Art in Australia

In Australia, the impact of modern art began to be felt in the late 1930s when threat of war brought some refugee and many expatriate artists to the continent. The work of individual artists showed the influence of modern movements such as Cubism, Futurism and Surrealism. Following the Second World War, increased contact with Europe led to the rise of two groups of artists, one based in Melbourne, the other in Sydney. One of the Melbourne group, Sidney Nolan, was the first Australian painter to achieve international recognition. Born in Melbourne in 1917, he was largely self-taught, showing an early interest in the technique of collage. Later, he became increasingly interested in Australian folk history, and developed a powerful folk-naïve style. His series of paintings of the notorious bushranger and folk hero Ned Kelly won him international fame. Their brilliant colours and bold, imaginative designs combine historical events with the stark and striking beauty of the Australian landscape.

African Art

In Africa, the new trends of painting and sculpture which emerged in the 1930s reflected a growing desire on the part of the Africans to be part of a larger, modern world. Artists like Ben Enwonwu (1921–) and Sekoto began to exhibit their works and the first art schools were established. Some artists were untrained, and explored different styles from the naïve paintings of the Desfossés School to the Cubist-inspired compositions of the Poto-Poto School. They experimented with media such as gouache on cardboard or coloured paper, depicting the everyday and ceremonial life of Africa.

Another group of artists were trained at art schools in Africa or Europe, and under Western influence attached more importance to painting, taking some themes from Western life and exhibiting their works in Europe and the USA as well as Africa. In sculpture, they tended to use materials and techniques common to traditional African art – wood carving, clay modelling, bronze and brass casting – but in recent years a younger generation of artists has begun to use advanced Western methods of welding figures and casting in fibreglass. Print-making, too, has become popular among the younger artists whose work is still Western-oriented in its use of materials and techniques, with subject matter ranging from pure abstraction to social commentary, or fantasy and dream.

Sadly, traditional African art – among the most intense and imaginative in the world – is vanishing with the lifestyles of the tribes that supported it. Nevertheless, the influence it had on artists of the early twentieth century can still be felt today.

Left A painting by the Nigerian artist Grillo which shows the influence of modern Western art in design and colour.

Left A modern stone sculpture by Chipungu Kraal of Zimbabwe.

Glossary

Abstract art   A work of art which has no recognizable subject and is purely an arrangement of shape, line and colour.

Art movement   The label given by art historians to a group of similar styles of art, linking them together by a series of common ideals.

Collage   A picture made up of bits of paper, fabric or any other material stuck to a support or ground such as canvas.

Cubism   A French school of painting, collage, relief, and sculpture initiated in 1907 by Picasso and Braque, which made natural forms into a multifaceted surface of geometrical planes.

Etching   A method of print-making in which a design is cut or bitten into a metal plate by acid.

Futurism   A literary and artistic movement that arose in Italy in 1909 to replace traditional aesthetic values with the characteristics of the machine age.

Impressionism   A movement in French painting developed in the 1860s mainly by Renoir, Manet, Pissarro, and Sisley, recording a fleeting image of the effects of natural light.

Kinetic art   A work of art, usually sculpture, with moving parts.

Lithography   A method of 'surface printing' in which a design is drawn on stone with a greasy crayon. The crayon repels water but allows ink to adhere.

Manifesto   A public declaration of the ideas and aims of an individual or group.

Modelling   A term which can be used to refer to either the shaping and building up of a pliable material such as clay or wax by a sculptor, or the way a painter uses light and shade to give the illusion of three-dimensions to a figure or object in a painting or drawing.

Mural painting   A painting on a wall or ceiling which may either be painted directly on to the surface or on to a panel or canvas which is then fixed to that surface.

Perspective   A linear system by which an illusion of depth is achieved on a two-dimensional surface, and by which space is organized from a fixed viewpoint.

Post-Impressionism   Term applied to various styles of painting which followed Impressionism and was first used to describe the works of Cézanne, van Gogh, and Gauguin in 1911. Post-Impressionists often distorted natural appearance for the sake of design or to express their own emotions.

Relief sculpture/sculpture 'in relief'   Sculpture which is not free-standing but which is carved or modelled from a flat or a curved surface.

Renaissance   An Italian term meaning 'rebirth', referring to the revival in the arts and learning which took place in Europe, especially Italy, during the period from c. 1300 to 1550.

Silk-screen   A method of print-making which uses a tool called a squeegee to force ink through a fine mesh screen on to a surface. The design may be either cut into a stencil or painted on to the screen in a waxy film.

Vorticism   An art movement in Britain initiated in 1914 by Wyndham Lewis combining the techniques of Cubism with the concern for the problems of the machine age shown in Futurism.

Further Reading

Cumming, R., **Just Imagine – Ideas in Painting** (Kestrel, 1982).
Januszczak, W., and McCleery, J., **Understanding Art** (Macdonald, 1982).
Lynton, N., **Looking at Art through the Ages** (Kingfisher, 1981).
Powell, J., **Painting and Sculpture** (Wayland, 1989).
Unstead, R. J., **Incredible Century: A Pictorial History 1901–70** (Macdonald, 1974).

Picture acknowledgements
The publishers have attempted to contact all copyright holders of the illustrations in this title, and apologise if there have been any oversights.

Works by the following artists appear by kind permission of: Max Ernst, Pablo Picasso, Kenneth Noland: © DACS 1989; Henri Matisse: © Succession Henri Matisse/DACS 1989; Georges Braque, Marcel Duchamp, Joan Miró: © ADAGP, Paris, DACS, London 1989; Kurt Schwitters: © COSMOPRESS, Geneva, DACS, London 1989; Malcolm Morley: courtesy of the Saatchi Collection, London; Duane Hanson: courtesy of OK Harris Work of Art, New York; Henry Moore: © Henry Moore Foundation 1989, reproduced by kind permission of the Henry Moore Foundation; Richard Hamilton: courtesy of the artist; Barbara Hepworth: courtesy of the Barbara Hepworth Museum, St Ives, Cornwall; Percy Wyndham Lewis: © estate of Mrs G A Wyndham Lewis; Francis Bacon: courtesy of the artist and the Granada collection; Sidney Nolan: courtesy of Roy Miles Fine Paintings, 3 Berkeley Square, London; Mark Rothko: courtesy of Christopher Rothko and Kate Rothko Prizel; Eduard Munch © Nasjonalgalleriet, Oslo.

The illustrations in this book were supplied by: BBC Hulton Picture Library 28 (bottom), 29 (top), 37 (top); The Bridgeman Art Library 6,7 (both), 8, 11 (bottom), 13 (bottom), 19 (top), 26 (left), 35 (bottom right), 44 (bottom); Michael Holford 13 (above left); Chapel Studios Picture Library, *frontispiece*, 43 (top left); Colin Taylor 32; Communist Party Picture Library 26 (right); David Cumming 24 (bottom); OK Harris 41; The Design Council 27 (top); Hutchison Library/Juliet Highet 45 (top); Imperial War Museum 20, 30 (top); Lee Miller Archives 14 (bottom); John Frost 19 (bottom); Mary Evans Picture Library 4, 17 (top), 30 (bottom); Museum of Modern Art, New York 12, 13 (top), 31; Namuth/Photri 33; National Gallery, Oslo 10; Paul Popper Ltd 44 (top); Philippe Halsman/Magnum 24 (above); Hutchison Library/Robert Aberman 45 (bottom); Roger Viollet 21 (both top), 25 (top); Ronald Sheridan 37 (bottom); Royal Academy of Arts 17 (bottom); Saatchi Collection, London 40; Science Museum 5 (both): Tate Gallery Archive 23,27 (bottom, Studio International), 34 (top right, Alexander Liberman), 35 (bottom left, M Hardy); Tate Gallery, London 14 (top), 15 (bottom right and top right), 16,18,22,25,28 (top), 29 (bottom), 34,36 (left); Tate Gallery, Liverpool 34 (bottom right); Tony Morrison 42; Topham Picture Library 15 (bottom left), 36, 39 (both), 43 (bottom); Victoria and Albert Museum 21 (bottom); Waddington Gallery 38.

Index

Page numbers in *italics* refer to illustrations.

Abstract Expressionism 32, 35
Action painting 32
Andre, Carl 42
Andrea, John de 40
Armory Show 19

Bacon, Francis 35, *35*
Balla, Giacomo 16–17, *16*
Baudelaire 6
Beuys, Joseph 39
Blue Rider, The 10, 26
Boccioni, Umberto 16–17
Body art 42
Brancusi, Constantin 15, *15*
Braque, Georges 13, *13*, 15
Breton, André 31
Bridge, The 9, 10

Cézanne, Paul 6, *6*, 8
Christo *43*
Close, Chuck 40
Collages 15, 26
Constructivism 26
Cubism 11, 13, 15, 19, 45

Dada 20–22
Dali, Salvador 24, *24*
De Stijl 27
Delaunay, Robert 15
Derain, André 8
Duchamp, Marcel 19, *19*, 21, 22

Enwonwu, Ben 45
Epstein, Jacob 15, *15*
Ernst, Max 23, *25*, 31, *31*
Expressionists 9–11

Fauves, Fauvism 8, 19
Freud, Sigmund 5, 23
Futurism 11, 16, 17, 20

Gabo, Naum 26
Giacometti, Alberto 35

Grillo *45*
Gris, Juan 15

Hamilton, Richard 38, *38*
Hanson, Duane 40, *41*
Happenings 39, 42
Hepworth, Barbara 28–9, *29*
Hockney, David 38, *39*

Impressionists 7

Kandinsky, Wassily 10, 26
Kaprow, Allan 39
Kinetic art 37
Kirchner, Ernst 9, *9*
Klein, Yves 39
Kline, Franz 32
Kraal, Chipungu *45*

Land art 42
Leger, Fernand 15
Lichtenstein, Roy 39

Magritte, René 23
Malevich, Kasimir 26, *26*
Manet, Edouard 6, *7*
Marc, Franz 10, *11*
Maria, Walter de 42
Marinetti, Filippo 16, *17*
Mathieu, George 35
Matisse, Henri 8, *8*
Mexican Muralists 44
Miró, Joan 23, *25*, 26
Mondrian, Piet 27, *27*, *31*
Moore, Henry 28, *28*, 29
Morley, Malcolm 40, *40*
Munch, Edvard 10, *10*
Muybridge, Eadward 17

Naïve art 43–5
Neoplasticism 27
Nolan, Sydney 44, *44*
Noland, Kenneth 36, *36*

Op art 37
Orozco, José 44

Paolozzi, Eduardo 39
Performance art 39, 42
Pevsner, Antoine 26
Picabia, Francis 21, *21*, 23
Picasso, Pablo 8, 12–16, *13*, *14*, *15*
Pollock, Jackson 32, *33*, 34, 35
Pop art 38–9
Post-Painterly Abstraction 38–9

Ray, Man 21
Renaissance 6, 12, 35
Riley, Bridget 37, *37*
Rivera, Diego 32, 44, *44*
Rothko, Mark 32, 34, *34*

Sand painting 32
Schwitters, Kurt 22, *22*
Sekoto 45
Severini, Gino 16
Siqueiros, David 44
Smithson, Robert 42
Stella, Frank 36
Superrealism 40
Suprematists 26, 27
Surrealism 23–4, 28, 31, 32, 44
Symbolists 12

Tanguy, Yves 31
Tatlin, Vladimir 26
Tzara, Tristran 21, *21*

Van Doesburg, Theo 27, *27*
Van Gogh, Vincent 10
Vasarely, Victor 37
Vlaminck, Maurice de 8
Vorticists 16

Warhol, Andy 38–9, *39*
Wols 35
Wyndham Lewis, Percy 16, *18*